About the Author

Riley Harris is a young, aspiring poet. She spends her days writing poetry and short stories, basking in the presence of nature, and dancing with her friends.

Words With Trees

Riley Harris

Words With Trees

Olympia Publishers
London

www.olympiapublishers.com
OLYMPIA PAPERBACK EDITION

A CIP catalogue record for this title is
available from the British Library.

ISBN: 978-1-80439-310-9

This is a work of fiction.
Names, characters, places and incidents originate from the writer's
imagination. Any resemblance to actual persons, living or dead, is
purely coincidental.

First Published in 2024

Olympia Publishers
Tallis House
2 Tallis Street
London
EC4Y 0AB

Printed in Great Britain

Dedication

For my favorite soulmate, my father and my soul, Josephine Keys, and lastly, my muse, Swan.

Acknowledgements

Thank you to my father, Ethan, for being my best friend and biggest supporter. Nothing in my life would be accomplished without his presence. Thank you to my twin flame, Josie. All that I know of the world and spirituality is thanks to her. I know the trees because I know her. Thank you to Amanda for pushing me to publish my work and being a great supporter of my poetry. I would have never put *Words With Trees* together if she hadn't said everything was attainable. Thank you to the universe for making everything as simple as sitting under a tree. Thank you to my brother, Hunter, for being my light in the dark and sitting with me to read most of these poems. Thank you to my many lovers. Thank you all for showing me I had a heart. Thank you for breaking it and mending it. Thank you, Kyle, Lachlan, Cicily, Josie (again), and Sammy. Thank you, Aubrey, Kiah, Ren, Jocelyn, Grace, and Carley for simply being my friends. Thank you to Olympia Publishing for making my dreams come true. Finally, thank you to Mallory. If it wasn't for Mallory's poetry, I would have never fallen in love with the art. She has begun this journey for me. I want her to know that. All of this is thanks to her and the love we shared then.

1.

Words With Trees

As the thunder rolled along with heavy drops of rain,
I ran to sit upon the tree that spoke in vibrations.
The rain pummeled my back and the Sky sang out in
Monstrous claps.

I began to cry on the bark and held tightly to the tree's neck.
My head laid on its nose, and I sobbed into its chest.
I wondered and asked,
Do you think whenever we hold in our tears one time,
They will burst out randomly months later?
I wondered and spoke,
What if the sky cries when we don't listen to its pleas?

The sky yells at us through thunder
And gets angry enough to throw lightning bolts.
Are we too busy with despair to pay it any mind?
What if the sky's sadness is what invites us to be emotional?
I have never truly felt poetic before,
Until now, here upon you.

2.

I wonder what emotions are hidden in silence:
The breaths in between casual conversations,
Stolen glances from two lovers by the spot
They spent their summers,
The staring contests of opponents of attraction.

What feelings subside under our noses
When we are doing nothing but searching for their answers?
How often do we fold our confessions into our minds,
So our match does not find our enveloped letters
We send them in our hearts?

I wonder if the leaves on the trees mimic our internal
Thoughts of pleasure? Are the trees our translators
When our tongues will not pick themselves up?
Oh, there are so many questions
About where our thoughts of lovers in silence disappear
Because, of course, they have been transferred somewhere.
We wouldn't have poets if they weren't.

3.

As I stared at myself in the mirror
With paint covering my legs and hands,
Fingering blueberries in my mouth,
Listening to my best friend's music,
I wondered if these moments
Existed simply for poets and artists alike.

Such beauties exist to be immortalized.
Life exists for artists.
What would life be like without a nicely sung tune?

4.

Josephine

I can never seem to describe how You make me feel
Until our legs are tangled
And our bodies are intertwined messily.
Even now, I don't quite know
What it is about you that feels so natural
- Like taking a sip of iced water.

You are refreshing and comforting and you feel like
How trees make me feel.
You are a direct ancestor of Mother Earth.
You are soft and kind and sensitive
And lovey
And I feel like molding into you
When you are near.

The stars in my veins seem to have your image
Sewn into the constellations.
You are delicate like the afternoon sunlight
Dancing on the tip of the tree's leaf.
You are like the hushed wind of a light breeze.
You are as generous as the sunlight
Hiding kindly behind a small, moving cloud.

I have never felt my emotions become
More confused and messy
Until you rub your finger lightly on my skin.
I do not know how to explain the limbo
Of romantic and platonic love that I hold for you
In the green glow at the center of my chest.

You initiate a thousand waves out of my sea of feelings.
I don't know if I will ever form the right words
To explain the tsunamis you create in my body.

5.

We are not only one lover.
We are a million versions of one lover.
We become a new lover
Each time we meet someone new to love.
A different part of ourselves is magnified
To become compatible with our new.
We are not the same as the last
Because we are no longer with their love
And that version of our own love.
We have evolved and grown for the new.

6.

It is one of those moments again:
The ones that exist in a loop of Forever.

The sun caressed the leaves of my reading tree.
It tickled the bark and weeds.
The droopy canopy became lit with new beginnings and
hope
And lovely prose for each new branch.
The birds sang tunes to their lovers which inspired me to
Write a little poem about you, tree.

7.

Have you ever felt someone else's soul so strongly beneath
Your own bones?
When they have completely grasped onto your full lifeline:
The energetic field you maintain.
The part of you that becomes reincarnated into a thousand
New lives.
Out of this singular life, you will only feel what touched you.
With no physical form, they have touched somewhere you
Rarely swipe your hand through.

It is the musician I cannot get out of my head with the voice
I will hear in my new lifetime.
It is the memory that will make me remember that I am a
Recycled soul
Because the Universe is proper and doesn't waste.
It is the soulmates I have met who have burned emotion
Into my core, strong enough to feel hatred and love.
It is the thing that folded around my passion.
It is the color that filled my life.
It is what evolved my soul and forced more growth and
More evolution.
It is the art I saw in the gallery that I may have painted a few
Thousand lives ago,
But I couldn't tell.

But I can still feel the words my soul spoke.
As bubbles of emotion rose.
The third eye even sighed in awe.
It is the known small things
That will stitch the aura for my next life.
It is this poem.

8.

I noticed it briefly, almost not at all.
But when you put your leg out, and I touched you,
I didn't think of sparks or flying stars at the time.
It took my departure
To realize something minor
Had stopped, changed, been stunted.
It reminded me that
We were together a time ago.
Although I think of it often,
It feels as if I do not think of it at all.

9.

Noon.

Amaterasu sits highly on her throne.
The clouds form around her silhouette,
Causing her shine to blanket around them.
Soft, gentle rays fall through my window.
I almost hadn't noticed the leaves
That were bathing in her generosity.
She peaks past the canopy to look me in the eyes.
Hello, little wanderer,
How beautiful you look today.

10.

I laid on the grass at midnight
And gazed into the eyes of the sky.
The stars appeared as mere specks
Like sugar I could scoop into a cup
And throw around like pixie dust.
I examined the stars closely,
Looking past their minimal size from earth
And more into how they shined,
Contrasting the jet back canvas they laid upon.
I imagined picking them up with my hands
And looking closer at their exterior.
I thought of humans:
How we are scattered on earthly canvas.
Then I noticed the clouds brushing:
It looked like a big cage
Wandering through the night sky.
Life becomes more beautiful every time I look at it.

11.

You and the trees are my muse – and by you and the trees,
I mean you're the tree outside my house,
And the peaceful one I saw at the park.
You're the ease in my soul
When I stare at the leaves on the branches,
And you're the whisper of secrets
That brushes the kindness from the air.
You're the bark I laid my head on
In the storm when I cried,
Sitting on the lap of the one We climb together.
You're the rain that settles on the
Green then yellow then orange of the leaves.
But most of all, you're the green
Of Summer when the sun smiles brightly
Because it's her season and her time.
Mostly, because green is my favorite color,
And you are my favorite color.
And you're my favorite tree.
And you're my favorite weather.
And I love you,
If you didn't know.

12.

I read a poem today about a tree,
And suddenly,
There was no tree.
There's never been a tree.
It's always been you.

13.

I feel funny and well.
How often does that happen?
I feel youthful in my young body.
I feel the vibrations of my soul
Attracting the good in the world.
And I feel like green and blue and
Like a Tree, like a yellow-leaved tree in fall
That reads in the corner of the library with a coffee
In hopes someone will notice my book
And say, "Hey, I read that book."
"Awe, really, did you like it?"
I feel like the gold ring I wear around my middle finger
That's attached to my lover in another state.
I feel like my favorite song
With the colors yellow and blue illuminating my soul,
Like the brightest neon sign for joy and hope.
I think today I am happy.
Today, I am happy.
What a funny thing to be.

14.

And I can see you.

Wrap my hands in silver lace and shine my eyes with his;
I have never felt more delicate in someone's arms.
I feel humane, like glass that will shatter if it is knocked.
I feel like a narcissus flower roaming the field of hope,
Finding my way to you eternally.

The sun shines brightly, reminding me of your smile.
Poems are etched into the blue sky when you are around,
And now, I am always reminded of the warmth I feel when
I'm sitting in the heat, roughly June, book in hand,
And I can look over, and I can see you.

15.

Dreams drifted
From the blue in the sky to the blue in my eyes.
I saw them differently,
Like cleaning foggy glasses with a silk handkerchief
Once used to bathe Moses
When he was found by the Pharaoh's daughter.
The same river flowed overhead,
Covered with pudgy clouds,
Like freshly showered baby hands.
I peaceably placed myself in her lap
While I stared at a tree further away,
Standing lonely in the field,
But its loneliness made it much more poetic,
Like a eulogy delivered for Earth
Before she has died.

16.

Sometimes Trees Forget to Say Sorry

You know I was that tree once:
Making beauty out of my sorrows
And writing panegyrics to my friends that left.

The friends I still admired, even though I pushed them away
With no written letters of my love while they were still here.
Because sometimes trees forget to say sorry,
And I didn't mean to be rude when I said,
I couldn't be around your lips
When you talked about your boyfriend.

But you have to understand,
Your leaves touched mine too kindly
To breathe any oxygen that wasn't yours.

17.

I see her pale pink lips touch your shoulder softly
And the gesture is so kind, so lovely,
That I dare cry for the beauty of your love,
But I do not let a tear gleam in the light.
Soon my heart begins to flutter from the drop of our hands
Many nights ago.

To see you be kissed is thrilling, to see you happy,
To see you *in love*, is to lose myself in love with you.
For you to see you dance with her quietly, making no show
Of grandness, but doing it all the same,
To demand attention with affection like we never did,
Like we will never do

To see me dance with you, in the mirror of life,
To see me silently peck your shoulder,
My dear, do you see her watch?
I look in your eyes as you nod, but say back to me,
Maybe she misses us. I nod.
Not us, mi corazon. You.

18.

My fiery heart spills resentment-colored ink
On the pages of poets I think could write a better poem
About you than I could.
And I don't know if you've loved someone
With fingertips that were made to type love letters that
Couldn't be matched,
Even if they were spoken in the language of the Romantics.
But I can still tear out my heart
And juice the blood from my veins onto pages that have
Been crumpled into balls
Because maybe I wouldn't let you read the innermost walls
Of my body,
Like hieroglyphics no one can understand but you and I.
And believe me, I know, you can love someone else,
And I know that she could be lovely.
I know that we weren't the best pair,
But god, chérie, you are my muse.
You are the center of my poems and short stories
And they encapture the feeling of my love for you,
That seems to stretch into an eternal longing,
As August breeds with September to give us October: the
Month of our death.
I know I shouldn't be falling to my knees at your funeral,
And I won't
Because there's always an empty seat in the back for the

silent Lovers
That have been gone too long to be mourning freshly with
the rest.
Because I, my love, have wept at your bedside, even when
You were sick of my broken heart.
Can they say that they have kissed your eyes in July and
made Love to your soul in August?
Can they say that your rotations around the sun crashed in
Giant waves in their stomachs,
Lurching every time friends may have wished them a happy
Day?
Because we all know I can't tell you how much you mean to
Me and the lovers prior to our creation.
Only the Universe can send my bottled messages to you
Now.
You should learn astronomy, and I should too because
maybe We've been here all along.
I just don't know how to read the map of the stars,
And maybe you just didn't know how to send letters to the
Heavens with your dreams.

19.

I'm going to remember the smell of your books and the
Taste of your mischievous thoughts.
I'll remember the tales of love you told to your friends.
I would kiss your dimples if you had them, but for now,
I can hopelessly ponder at the pond of infatuation I created
For you.
The Willow and I will discuss your sarcastic demeanor that
Makes me feel like you know more about life, and I only
Have so much to learn.
Once I've mapped out the movement of the clouds on the
Day of your funeral,
I will call you 'morrow, and we can kiss again before your
Greeting with Cerberus.
The Willow laughed when I told her your name because I
Ring in a tune of love you can't reach yet.
One day, you will, and I'll be waiting on our star.
I'll send suns on bows every night so you can wish for me
Like I wish for you.

20.

I'm trying to remember how I felt before you came back.

I know that I was dating and trying to love everyone
In some way near the bounds of love,
But not close enough to drown in pools of admiration.
I know that I was seeing people left and right
Forming relationships with strangers on bus rides.
I know that I hadn't kissed anyone in over a month
Because I didn't even try to kiss a new admirer.
I know that I was singing love tunes to the trees
And taking walks every day.
I know that I was reading a book about love mending
Wounds and creating more over time.

I just need to know if you were mixed in thought.
Where were you in my brain?
Obviously, you were there.
But were you hidden under a pile of books?
Were you reading my journal entries in the right part of my
Mind?
Where had you gone for all of this time,
And how often did my mind decide to think of you?
I wish I could remember where you were stored
Because now that you're unwrapped and out of the package,
It's like you've always been here

Beside me with a mug full of Love tea.

Maybe I'm still dreaming.
You don't seem real.
Are you real?
Kiss me again, so we can find out.

21.

Hair that burns quietly like a silent storm,
Dark clouds of gray that have poems within their tears,
Falling into the mortal world –
You are everything of the gods.

Prometheus sent you to us as a token of sincerity
Because how could we live without your existence?
Your laugh is a noise that could save Earth from ashes,
And your presence is as if I were dining with Selene.
You are knotted into the core of a tree,
And I am jealous of your fittings into Nature.

Persephone and Artemis hold your hands tightly around
Theirs,
Springing cherry blossoms on your arms and drawing yellow
Peonies in your heart.
You are the center of baby blue in my world, and you have
The passion of purple poppies.

22.

The dark leaves fell around the awning of trees, and I
pictured you crying in bed.
Tears ruining the pretty makeup you fussed over earlier, and
only I would know how much you did.
I screamed toward the deep red leaves, reminding me of the
carnelian heart in your chest.
Why did you let me hold your anatomical heart when I only
drew you valentine's hearts?
Why did I hurt the most beautiful girl I know because I love
someone else?
And how do I give you my love without pouring my blood
on your lips?

23.

Wine red is the color of my language,
And my tongue speaks in quiet whispers of love,
Always calling out to your soul.
Like the light spring breeze,
I'll shake lightly like the trees,
As the wind caresses the green on their leaves,
I'll moan when your hands peer into the windows
Of my soul that is molding into yours eternally.
Whisper loudly to me in the words of poetry,
And I can give you my hand in the touch of love.

24.

Lover of Swans

The Goddess of Love shone brightly overhead,
Aura seeping into the gloomy air,
Changing the gray clouds to a pastel pink.
And I thought of the way you smiled at me with eyes of
love, And I wished I could confess this to Aphrodite,
But I'm afraid to let your name leave my mouth
Because that would mean I would have to admit,
My soul is wrapped around the body of a boy
That doesn't like the sound of my voice anymore.
Or maybe you do? Do you?
That's not important anymore, I suppose.
The only importance is this: I love you, and She knows.
And I will tell her over and over
Until she sends Eros on a journey to your heart.
I'll walk hand-in-hand with Aphrodite to meet the lovers I
Missed,
Because she wants me to know that I could unlove you if I
Wished,
And Eros found a bow meant for someone that wasn't you.
But then, well, I wouldn't be me If I didn't love you,
So, I will decline her offer,
And she will tell me that there's no reason to send Eros to
Your bedroom door

Because they found love for me stored
In the pits of your chest along with hope and patience.
So, my love,
Veni. Vidi. Amavi.
Will be written on my headstone next to yours along with
Lover of Swans.

25.

Down to the sweat dripping from the heavens,
I called out to you in a sea of allusions to our love.
Remember when I was buried in the tree?
I was digging beneath the earth and you kissed my eyelids
And flipped over my body and kissed the rest of me,
And I kept digging a hole that smelled of lavender
And crying on my floor with my colored lights shining.
I straddled your waist and moaned into your ear
Which is a new memory for me, and I would do it again
If it meant you would move my body, too.
Do you recall admitting that you loved me again and again
Into the space between our gravitational lips?
This is a new memory for me, and I want to keep calling out
from the void between us.
I'll go back in time when I cried on my green satin sheets
That are still untouched by your nudity.
I'll transfer my memory into the dreams of June and July,
And I'll have to see you at work,
And I'll think about your fallen head that I nearly slain with
My hands gripping.
And I bet that you would let me, if I wanted to.
I bet you'd let me kill you.
But I won't because you'd be gone then,
And I at least need you for the rest of time.
So, I can call out to you for an eternity.
I can't ever imagine unloving you.

26.

Trees that could ease the turmoil of the soul drifted into a
Soft sleep,
As fairytale creatures spread the word of lost love across the
Forest
And whispers told of forbidden likeness between the moon
And the koi fish.
Meaning between you and my heart, swept the stars under
The rug of the black sky.
The blazing suns blew up to ten times their size as I dreamt
Of green leaves turning dark red,
And I dreamt of kissing a girl you and I both know instead
of Kissing your lips,
And I wondered if the trees would tell you, for you are the
Greatest energy on our planet.
But I can't help but be pulled to you,
And I apologize that my dreams lead my heart in different
Directions sometimes,
But you're here and I'm here,
And I wouldn't want to lick any other lips.
Sometimes, though, I dream of your hair tangled into
Someone else's fingers,
And my burning yellow soul gets extinguished by the loss of
Your heart,
Even if it's in my dreams.
These trees never lie, so don't be alarmed when they express

That I tell the moon about you,
And sometimes the sun can feel the burning love inside of
My beating heart.
Her golden glow paints yearn for my soul when I sit in the
Spotlight of Earth's set,
And I remember your love also painting feelings on my
Complexion.

27.

Your blonde hair reminds me of the willow,
And your thoughts are somewhere deep within the core of
The earth.
Maybe you're a mountain, but I've most definitely seen you
As a tree.
Somewhere alone but never lonely.
Somewhere quiet with profound thoughts so loud.
Somewhere green like winter on pine trees.
Where have you been?
And to what life will you go after?
A recycled soul dispersed into all times in the cosmos,
Existing in every timeline,
Lodged into the world as a part of nature.
Are you a tree? I can't tell.
Something tells me you are now.

28.

I Learned from the Trees

Did you forget the color of red that tainted my valentine's cards?
Because I would never forget the crimson-colored February that is to be spent in your arms every day.
I would never forget the dark blue in the depths of the ocean when you were gone for a year,
And I constantly wondered if I'd ever get to tell you I love you again, maybe once or twice, preferably a dozen.
This rotation around the sun, I can put glitter on your cards and buy you bears to hug when I'm not around.
I will write you poems every day because Love, this is your time. The rest of our lives are meant to be spent loving each other and loving the rain and new books and tea that stains our night table and our favorite wine.
Because when I'm with you, the green on the trees is more viridescent than usual. Even when it's winter, I can see the outline of Us on the willows.
They whisper names of love with their vibrations, sending affectionate notes to the Universe like I do to you
Because where do you think I learned how to love?
I learned from the trees, and I get to use my heart on You.

29.

I remember it all on a hazy film camera,
With grain marks covering your luscious lips that kiss the
inner corners of my mouth,
Where you sipped my spit like your favorite tea and I asked
if you'd sip the blood from my veins ,
Because I wanted as much of myself inside of you as you
had of yourself inside of me.
See, I find you in the way I dress and talk. You're in the
movements of my hands,
And you are laced into the moans of my touchings. I could
call out your name with my silence
Because you are the loudest vibration that I can feel. Now
that all is dead and void between us,
Sometimes I'll spit on my fingers and lick them seductively
for I have a desperate need to become you,
to fold into you, to lose myself inside of you,
to forget my own words and have them all be yours,
so that I can write myself letters with your thoughts.

30.

Words are deep and personal
When they strike the heart the right way,
When they whimper down the streams of one's own veins
And creep into the core center of our souls:
The colorful spot where my heart seeps into energy.
Words can prick this spot with a deep red pool of love,
Like my heart was bleeding with the mere admiration of
These words.
These words I want to kiss and hold and mold into
Like I am a flowing ball of lava or a distant star
Or rooted beneath the beautiful tree outside my window.
These altruistic words are buried into my being
And exude such love that the only words I can hear him
Mutter are, I want you to love me until you die.
I want you to love me longer than that.
I sobbed into myself, folding my chin into my chest,
Feeling the drums of my aliveness beat on my crying cheeks
As I said to no one but the emptiness of my room,
Please pull me into you,
I want to fit between your knees
And bury myself inside of you,
And Burrow into the beating eye of your chest.
I can feel my entire body shake with love for you,
And I would sooner die than not feel your affection.

31.

With the deceiving parts of my branches visible,
I waver with the wind as it passes through my viridescent
Leaves.
Can you see me? I yell out to the wandering sky.
The blue face sometimes lies behind the clouds of secrets
While I yearn for a drop of its sadness to quench my thirst.
I only need you to cry, dear sky, bring me an emotional fury,
Please fuel the invisible half of myself.
My roots are planted further beneath the earth than the
Holes you dig, and I cannot seem to find any water for my
Tears.
I am screaming out for love.
Show me love, dear sky, bring me your kindness in the form
Of drops in the eye.
I need to laugh with the storm winds and yell with the
Howling coos.
I want to rip myself apart with you.

32.

She lay motionless on the softened moss where I sometimes
Lay my head,
Thinking of her fingertips as they danced upon the center
Of my chest.
Her gaze was a melted pool of love, with eyes that sought
After your secrets,
Finding them, at long last, in knotted ribbons of kindness.
Her head was toward the sky: the azure, beautiful sky.
She molds my heart with her hands even when she is silent
And looking away.
Lovely is what her name used to be before she was given an
Earthly body,
And I am the only lover she has held in her arms, soft and
Naked like a bubble bath – in which I end up sobbing,
My cheeks redden with my salted tears and her thumb is
There to rub them away.
Fully in love, I smiled through tears at the whiteness of her
Dress and the purity of her soul,
And I would be pink if she wanted me, or yellow or blue,
Even gray to please her.

33.

I wanted to be fake.
A mere echo of a name in someone's mouth.
I yearned to be the lie on his tongue.
Do not tell the truth
When I kiss you with my eyes closed.
In my head, you will kiss me back
Delicately, like your soul is ascending
Further into mine,
Like I am alive for this moment
And you knew it would happen,
But you would not say
Because you needed my free will to be here,
My lips on your lips,
My tongue sliding past our barriers.
For a moment, I could feel the softness of his skin,
The peach fuzz on his face,
And for a moment, it was not fake.
When his hands wrapped themselves around mine,
I dared to stop time,
Here and now, I am stopping it.
Freezing it.
Framing it in my mind.
His hands were pastels painting on my fingers
As they grazed my skin,
And then I was delicate.

For a moment, I did not think it was fake,
And then I wished if it were fake,
I wanted to be fake.

34.

Mother of My Art

You are my river,
Flowing to the ocean of my enlightenment.
You are the hand that I write with, creating my poetry.
You give birth to the thought in my mind,
You are pregnant with my children, smiling brightly with
Beads of sweat, as the crowning of my own thoughts leaves
Your thighs.
You are the knife to my wrist
That looks at me with a silver reflection and cries,
Halt the breath with my blade if you aren't scared,
But is there not someone that would cry even louder than
The sadness inside your beating chest?
You are the trees and bubbling brook where I mediate.
You are my love.
The deepest emotion I have felt
Has been from your soul
Stepping poetically against mine.

35.

Here I am,
Deflated, saddened, flat, pressed
Against the pages of my poetry
To decorate my heart for you.
I want you to like it here.
I can bring you tea and kiss your forehead
And baby you like the other half of my soul.
I want to fall on your skin
With my nudity and sculpt myself
Around your own body.
I know you could hear me from the moon.
You would know if I died on the sun,
And I would know if you wanted to die with me.
I could give you hemlock on my casket
Because I could not imagine the afterlife
Without your precious soul.
Your skin is familiar to me like my own.
I would paint you in the dark.
I know your marks better than myself.
I know your heart better too
Which means I have lived here longer than you.
You know me more than the trees,
And I tell the trees about you,
So, fall with me
Into the darkness and light the way

Because you are the lighter parts of my life.
You are the window with no curtains.
You are my hope.
You are my moon.
You are my lover.
No matter where I am,
I am here with you.

36.

The sun whispered through the curtains,
Did they kiss you like you hoped?
I think she recalled the last I spoke to her, when I found
your name in the clouds.
Her light fondled my fingers and sweater,
Will you tell your lover that you love?
She felt as though she knew the answer, but she seemed to
ask me anyway.
I sighed and told her about the night I kissed your bruised
knuckles and calloused hands.
The sun laid warmth on my lips,
What happens when love dies?
A curious look fell on my face and laughter fell from those
lighted lips.
"You would know, Amaterasu."

37.

Hello, Darling.
How did you sleep?
I hope that it was well and you dreamt of holding hands
with the trees.
I hope that you have been kind to Earth, and she has been
the dearest to you.
I hope that your pillows are softer and your blankets are
warmer.
I hope that your heart feels gentle and your soul feels like a
sprouting flower.
I hope that your home has become your favorite place.
And lastly, I hope your body has become your sacred temple.

38.

the sticky goo of my insides stuck my heart to the chopping board,
beating, alive and well, more proof that i am human.
my heart beats the same as yours. my heart beats when i am sad. my heart beats when i yell.
my heart beats when i laugh. and my heart beats now,
when i am covering my eyes with my mittens dry-heaving about the loss of my love.
i pick up my knife
and make contact with my heart. the twinge in my chest aches,
and i hold my hands to the center. has loss ever felt so heavy before? once a third of it is split,
i hand him his slice. here, for letting me love you.
now and tomorrow and for eternity, I have loved you.
nothing has changed and nothing will change, but we have changed.
love can grow and sprout into something new, but this next part is without you.
so here, take this to reminisce.
and never ever forget me.

39.

Even if you leave me Alone,
In the beat of my heart
And the voice of my breath,
God will find you.

And by God, I mean Love.

40.

So, when the sun smiles and light hits my eye,
Blinding my sight for a moment,
I will look inward
And I will feel

Love.
Pure Love.
Like a liquid vibration that I can drink
And stir with my tongue.

41.

Existence is temporary on this earth,
But what a lovely way to spend a few decades
With the trees waving hello to me in the spring
And the birds chirping as I open a book on the grass.
I have kissed so many lovers.
I wonder if I remember the taste of their lips.
I can dance and feel music course through my veins
Like the sun has taken my pulse and made it brighter.
I touch the skin of my friends
And give them my love through my fingertips.
There are drawings I have seen,
Sculptures I have admired,
And art I have loved.
There are humans too!
With bodies like no other
And voices that can say I love you
Or I hate you,
Or please don't go.
We can sing songs and laugh because we're so happy.
We can yell and cry and smile,
And we can love and love again and love again,
And love and love and love as many times as we please.

42.

My poems remember the day I cried in the woods, and they
remember sitting alone,
Listening to the sound of frozen trees screaming for the
sunlight,
Screaming for the love in the warmth.

I watched your footsteps trail away, and I silently cried
because I didn't want you to hear.
But now,
I would scream my tears ensuring they would reach your
ears.
I would carve my heart into the tree to show you the
rawness of my soul
And the reality of my words.

My poems miss loving you,
But losing you is something like love.

43.

sometimes there's all that needs to be: you and me.
and the tree.

44.

I see you
Near the heart-shaped pond.
Your voice moves silently and I want to tell you to speak
Louder
But your hair wisps in your face and I quietly ask the wind to
Remove your body from your soul
So I can read the colors of your aura.
How, my love, can your lips move in this spring warmth
When there is this pond, I have no thoughts.
But you and your brain are unstoppable,
So, I tell my body to change into a frog
For her ducks I croak and smile,
But you can't see
Because if you truly wanted to be with me, you would
drown Your human form
And tell it to live as the heartbeat in my chest.
I would put my hand over your being and tell you secrets at
Nighttime
But now you only smile at me with an arrow in your spine
So, I smile back because of this heart-shaped pond
And the thought of leaving you

45.

Let us Live, for we must Die.

The landscape opened to the garden of love:

Butterflies flew over the heart-shaped pond, and hyacinths
walked on the same path as me.

Together were we, standing so closely.

My breath was pink like the morning fog of our woods, and
your eyes glistened when you saw my blue aura turn green
when your skin grazed my arm.

And my fingers were like vines twisting up your body, eager
to know the deep secrets of your human form.

Is this Heaven? I heard you ask the tree when you walked
away from me.

I noticed the Universe open into a black hole, and I was not
frightened

For beauty was glorious and poetic enough to kill me
mercilessly

And I loved all that never said Sorry for existing.

So, you see, you and I, we must live,

For we will die within seconds of our breath's departure.

So, kiss me with your tongue and love me with your words
and mold me with your soul,

and after eternity, our souls will ring

in this garden of love.

46.

a pink fog dispersed over my bed as she descended wearing
white: angel or lover?
both?
her lips were glossed, and if I looked closely,
I could see my name beneath her skin glowing like a lamp
beneath a planet of human body.
suddenly, I was taken to the sky (the ceiling)
and she was lying where I rest
where I rest and dream of her, where I rest and think of her,
where I rest and want her,
she laid in my space like a fairy, her hair gathered around her
with lilies falling into the blonde "do,"
her voice was a faint whisper and I closed my eyes to hear
but that meant I could not see her beauty, so I chose to turn
off every sense
and give myself to her, molding into her soul, hearing the
beat of her breath
listening to the vibration of her vocals, "you miss me?"
ache, a crack in my chest, I could hear the tree fall,
and I could see her blue and cold
like nighttime fears.

47.

On the Side of Peace and Love,
I can grow my flowers in my soul and smile at the trees
While not far off,
The trees are dying with the people like a sacrificial
Bloodshed
For the economy
Like a dictatorship on a rock
Like the wrong note played at the concert where the
Audience will not speak up – they want the piano played
No matter if it is correct, play the piano
Make our money worthwhile
Show us your play of war
Show us how you bomb our people
Show us with no remorse
We will do nothing but clap
And say again,
This Is The War To End All Wars.
But in the back, I see the garden
I see the waterfall with people crying
With their signs that say Make Love Not War,
And there is where I belong,
On the side of Peace and Love.

48.

You whisper to me through this fruit
And I can see your face like my dream last night
Where your mother led you up the stairs
And I thought we could talk,
But I was gone too soon.

Through this fruit now,
I can tell you that I miss you
And your voice saying I understand is vivid
Like your tears in the woods.
And suddenly, I wish I was the snow you walked on that day
But sadly, I am only the heart
That told you I couldn't hold yours anymore.

Say my name to the trees when you miss me.
They will send your message through the roots,
And I will sit on the earth
And live through the soil to find you.

49.

Leaves gather around my head
Like hair wisped into my face by the wind
Bark covers my skin as a vulnerable place mat
And I, tree, try to climb the sky
To see the world, to look for you,
To find you in the blanket of the wind,
To push away the leaves.
Searching for you from this branch,
I could see you,
If I tried, I could notice you,
I could look at you and stay silent
Because there is nothing to say with words,
But much to say with my eyes.
I have turned you into art in my mind
And I wanted to see if you would look nicely against the
brown of my bark,
But also, to ensure that you are real
And if you still exist out there
Because sometimes, I would like to see you.
You can sit under my canopy
And I will send you poetry through my roots.

50.

I felt the universe on my skin,
Like the sun was sharing a secret with me
about the coupling of seasons

Did you mean to make me feel so close?
I touched the tree with my fingers
But really, my soul was seeping into the bark
and I could feel the soul of the tree on my skin

Oh, to have a body and feel the beauty of life with my
hands, I can touch love with my nose,
I can smell honeyed colors in the air with my ears,
I can hear the breath of my beloved

I can tell you that I could feel the earth without touch,
But isn't a body meant for touch?
Shouldn't I hug the body of my trees and kiss the ground
like it deserves?
Shouldn't I drink the brook to have it stream through me as
if my own blood was made from its water?
From this time, I am the brook
and my blood is clear like the air in spring

For a moment, I am spring
I am heaven personified
I am the voice when the tree can't speak
I am

51.

I have the reddest heart for love.
For human beings, I bleed in the kindest ways.
With kisses, I am showing them that I want their lips to
touch mine, to remember this, to remember them.
I give them poetry in my smile, in my dance, in my
invitation. Blood the color of fire, Blood to drown their
sorrows,
Blood to share, to mend, to cure.

But for you, my heart is green
Like the color of the trees, my favorite color, it shines like
the sun in vibrations of Love.
Love is delivered to you in my commitment to you.
Without you even knowing, I have vowed myself to be
yours. Make me your globe, make me your song,
Strum my words on your guitar.

Let me be green for you.
Forget the red of love.
Let me be the color of the Earth.

52.

Quiet breath breathing like the wind at dusk,
Your hazed eyes are darker in the shadows, hidden from the
sun, found by the moon
The silent nod of an unspoken understanding, you see me,
my moon, and I know you do
And I see you eternally, like a subconscious voice. Did the
whispers of daylight scare you away?
You hide in the nighttime, only to be shown the darkness of
my heart,
But I will give you the sun's light, I will hold you with the
beauty of a lover's lip,
With the gentleness of a murmuring stream, with the
loveliness of your own existence.

Folded, am I, like a swan sauntering across the pond to see
the joy of daylight at last
When what once was a dream is now a reality, when what
once was sleep is now aliveness,
When what was once my own fantasy is now.
The meeting of you and me is like a nebula, with a purple
cloud that calls out to you
On a frequency that only I can hear.

In the sky, away from Earth,
You are somewhere among this vast space that was lit by

nothing but the moon
Until I saw the nebula and you, until I felt the aliveness of
your smile, of your laugh,
I knew then that there was more to the galaxy than the
moon because if life be the moon, then you are more
You are more than a poem, more than a song, more than art
itself,
You are the embodiment of all the universe.

Within a single glance from you, I am under a spell that
existed before I had choice
Where is free will when there is you?
What is fate if it is not for us?

Do you hear the quiet breath breathing like the wind at
dusk? Am I mistaking you for nature again?
You always seem so close to the trees to me.